THOMAS ALVA EDISON: WHO WAS HE?

GOLU KUMAR

Copyright © Golu Kumar
All Rights Reserved.

This book has been published with all efforts taken to make the material error-free after the consent of the author. However, the author and the publisher do not assume and hereby disclaim any liability to any party for any loss, damage, or disruption caused by errors or omissions, whether such errors or omissions result from negligence, accident, or any other cause.

While every effort has been made to avoid any mistake or omission, this publication is being sold on the condition and understanding that neither the author nor the publishers or printers would be liable in any manner to any person by reason of any mistake or omission in this publication or for any action taken or omitted to be taken or advice rendered or accepted on the basis of this work. For any defect in printing or binding the publishers will be liable only to replace the defective copy by another copy of this work then available.

Contents

CHAPTER ONE

We will need to travel across the Atlantic and to America to witness the greatest investor of all time when he was a young lad. Because she is a daughter of the ancient Mother Country, New England, as we call her, is where we must turn for brightness and a sharpness of wit that occasionally reminds us of the flash of polished steel. England has accomplished wonders in the way of discovery and invention.

We are all familiar with Edison. It is not a name from history because he is still alive and in his prime today, producing marvels from his mamarvelousrain that continue to astound people and earn him the moniker "wonder-worker of the modern world."

As I type, I can see a square, brick home with exterior shutters that are hooked back, a white paling partially surrounding it, and a few barren, leafless trees in front of it. The house is simple and run-down, and to our English eyes, it looks curiously unfamiliar, but it is of the utmost interest to us because it is where Thomas Edison was born.

The boy first saw the light in 1847, and although the entered the world with only a memeagerupply, he was received with an abundance of love and affection. Mrs. Edison was a mother in a million and had Scottish blood in her veins. History frequently reveals that a son inherits his grandeur and many of the highest traits from his mother, and this son certainly inherited many of his from Mrs. Edison. During those formative years of his life that had such a profound impact on the "afterward, she was his constant companion, his adoring nurse, and his gentle teacher.

The child was seven years old when the Edison family moved to a place called Port Huron, and there he began to spend every spare moment reading. So earnest was he that he set himself to read through the Detroit Free Library, and had devoured a close row of volumes before his attempt was discovered.

Strange and solemn sosoundsome of the titles of the books he read when he was twelve years old--a time when most boys are lightly dipping into newspapers and magazines and books of adventure. Burton's _Anatomy of Melancholy_, Hume's _History of England_, Gibbon's _Decline and Fall of the Roman Empire_.

In 1862, when he was barely fifteen years old, he came out more fully from the shelter of home and mixed with the busy world, making a place in it for himself by his wits. He was a newspaper boy, and sold his papers like other boys, not stopping still in one place, but going on the train to different stations along the line, and selling as he went.

Around this time, America had a severe fever and ferment. People waited impatiently for word of each engagement as the North and South engaged in combat. Reports were eaten as soon as they were printed inonapers.

Now, Edison reasoned, "is my chance," and a grand scheme started to take shape in the young man's head. He went to the station telegraph clerk to start carrying it out.

He added, "I will promise you some papers, and now and then a magazine if you will allow me to wire the war news on a few stations ahead, and have it printed up on the blackboard."

He repeated his request to the different clerks along the line. His eager face and twinkling eyes and earnest words won all hearts, and his request was granted. He next went to the editor of a well-known paper.

"Give me a thousand copies," he begged, "and I will pay out of the proceeds of my venture." Here, again, he succeeded. And now it remained but to get the engine driver to promise him a few minutes at the different stations, and he started on his venture.

At the first stopping-place, he had been wont to sell some half-dozen papers. That day, as he looked out, the platform was strangely crowded, and it suddenly dawned on him, from the eager faces of the people and their exciting gestures, that it was _papers_ they wanted! He dashed onto the platform, and in a few minutes had sold forty at five cents each, or about a penny of our money. It was much the same at the next station. The people had read the headings on the station blackboard, and they crowded onto the platform, and the excited, hustling mob, for papers! It dawned on the boy, that there was a chance to raise his prices, so he doubled them, and sold 150 where he had used to sell a dozen! It was the same all along the line. At the last station--Port Huron--his home, the people were most excited of all. The town was a mile from the station. Edison started with his papers but was met halfway by an eager, hurrying crowd. They all wanted news. He stopped, drawing up in front of a church where a prayer meeting was being held. Presently the people poured out and surrounded the boy, willingly paying him five times the usual price of his paper. He began "to take in," as he expressed it, in his own terse, telling words, "a young fortune."

After this, the busy boyish brain began to look eagerly ahead, to face life seriously. He did not start on a fresh tack. He took hold of what was nearest to his hand, and he bent his mind on improving that. He had found people were in a hurry for news. The quicker they got it the better they were pleased. Nothing could surely be quicker than that they should get it damp from the press! So it flashed into his brain--why not print a paper on the train?

The question was no sooner asked than answered.

He looked about till he lighted on an old car, and he rigged it up as a printing office with old types and stereos he begged from a newspaper office. In this novel press-room, he threw off sheet after sheet of what he called _The Grand Trunk Herald_, the first and last paper ever printed on a train. The boy of fifteen was editor, compositor, and newsvendor in one. The paper "caught on," and the circulation went up to 400.

But, alas! misfortune was soon to overwhelm the young adventurer. One unlucky day the printing office--the old car, which grew daily more decrepit and unequal to the jolting of the journey--by a more violent lurch than usual threw over a bottle of phosphorus. The cork flew out, and in a few seconds, the car was in flames. They were easy enough to get under, but Edison's venture had received its death blow. The furious car conductor would henceforth have none of him. He boxed his ears and pitched him onto the platform along with his precious belongings--the whole paraphernalia of his craft.

It is a sorry picture that presents itself to our mind's eye. The boy standing half stunned, the rubbish and _débris_ of his belongings strewn at his feet, and the cherished old jolting car, the scene of his labors, gradually fading into the distance! It seemed as if his bright dreams were all extinguished, his golden hopes doomed to come to nothing. As he stood there he faced it all--a mere boy low down in the world, badly fed, poorly clothed, almost penniless, but we do not hear that he either flinched or complained or that a boyish sob rose in his throat. He was made of the stuff of the Stoic. It is our hearts that are sore and anguished, not chiefly for the hopes and dreams disappointed, but because of a terrible calamity that befell him then, when he was perhaps hardly conscious of it; but that grew darker and weightier as the years rolled on.

When the irritated conductor had boxed the boy's ears, so brutal had been his onslaught that the delicate nerves were injured for life, and now with the flight of years has come deafness to wrap the great inventor in a partial mantle of silence. It is perhaps we who feel most the infinite pathos of the thing, while the man himself bears his affliction with the same noble patience with which he accepted disappointment long years ago as a boy.

He immediately fearlessly turned his gaze back home at that point. He gathered his priceless possessions and transported them to his father's home's cellar.

Around this time, the Telegraph—a subject that has always piqued his curiosity throughout his life—started to occupy his thoughts. He had a great desire to excel in it as soon as he woke up. Despite being friendless and poor, he was adamantly, unwaveringly determined to succeed. So, using his little earnings from his job as a newsboy, he bought a book on telegraphing, which he studied day and night.

And now at this early age, I think the great inventor must have touched that mine that was afterward to yield him so wondrously of its wealth.

The boyish mind was putting out feelers, gropingly at first, in the direction of creation, that divine faculty that is granted to so few of us. We can recognize the seed in its first tiny sproutings. He and a boyfriend resolved to make a telegraph. They made a line of wire between their houses, insulated with bottles, and crossed under a busy thoroughfare using an old cable found in the bed of the Detroit River. The first magnets were wound with wire and swathed in ancient rags, and a piece of spring brass formed the key. Edison pressed two large and formidable-looking cats into his service, tied a wire to their legs, and applied friction to their backs. But the experiment failed. The cats, frightened and furious, resented the liberty, and parted company with, the wire, dashing off in different directions.

But failure never discouraged Edison, nor stayed the working of his brain. He was a true philosopher, and he was, like an elastic ball, possessed of enormous rebound.

Handed down to us there is a story of the boy which, while it may not throw much light on his brain, throws some on his heart and his ready courage. He was still a newspaper boy on the trains, and while at most stations a few minutes was the limit of waiting, at a certain station where shunting took place the minutes ran to half an hour. The boy was wont to spend this half-hour with the stationmaster's child, of whom he was fond, or to loiter about his garden. On this particular day, the engine driver had unlinked the cars in a siding, and one was being sent with a good deal of impetus to join another portion. It came on steadily, no one on it to control it, and right in its path was the unconscious baby smiling in the morning sunshine. Not a moment was to be lost. Edison threw down his papers and his hat on the platform and dashed to the rescue. And not a second too soon. As he threw himself and the child free of the line the car passed and struck his heel. The two fell with such violence on the gravel beyond that the stone particles were driven into their flesh, but they were safe!

The appreciative father was unsure of how to express his gratitude to the person who saved his child. He had little money and nothing to offer as payment. A strategy finally came to him.

He promised the youngster that he would teach him how to telegraph and get him ready for a job as a night operator, which would pay at least $25 a month.

Edison was quite happy. The agreement was reached. The child undoubtedly thought the wage—which was more than five of our English pounds—was a little fortune.

And now, even if it was only on the lowest round, he had his "toe on the tape" and his foot on the ladder. He could teach his teacher in three months, and he received the promised scenario. From then, he moved on to other circumstances, and over time, he started to leave his mark.

His thinking was incredibly quick to recognize a challenging issue and provide a solution.

There is a story told of how one winter a severe frost had coated the great river between Port Huron and Sarnia, how the cable was broken, and people could neither get news nor send it to the opposite bank of the river. The spot was crowded with people, baffled and vexed. Edison came along with a brain rarely at fault and faced the thing. Suddenly, to the onlookers' astonishment, he mounted a locomotive and sent a piercing whistle across the water, imitating by the toots of the engine the dots and dashes of the telegraph system.

In this manner, he yelled:

"Sarnia, holla! How do you understand me, Sarnia?"

The telegraph worker across the canal first remained silent. The excitement on the bank left everyone gasping for air. Finally, the unequivocal response was wonderful. The man on the other end had come around, and now the two cities could resume their "conversation."

After this, people began to hear of Edison's fame. But the mania for experiments had seized him. The cut-and-dried monotonous routine of work seemed flat and stale to him by comparison. It was as if an enchanted region of fairyland had been opened to the boy. To be allowed to revel in it he denied himself food and necessary sleep. When he was seventeen years old he invented a telegraph instrument that would transfer writing from one line to another without the help of an operator.

There was no want of openings now for him to choose from, but sometimes doors, after they had been opened, were rudely shut again through envy and evil feeling. In the great world of invention and discovery, there are perhaps more "ups and downs" than in any other. Some of Edison's fellow workers were kind and generous--others were jealous and detracting. One manager did him an ill turn. He was unequal to completing a discovery he had begun. On the thing being shown to him, Edison immediately "saw a light" and brought it to completion, but jealousy crept into the man's small mind and he dismissed the boy on a false charge.

So at seventeen, he was thrown again into the world. Money was still scarce. Books and instruments and calls from home swallowed up most of it. The boy was chafing under ill-treatment and a sense of injustice. The want of sleep, perhaps of proper food, was telling on him, but he looked forward with a clear, undaunted eye. He wanted to reach a certain town where he believed work awaited him. It meant a walk of a hundred miles. He was weak, disheartened, and ill-prepared for it, but he did it. He arrived footsore and weary, with torn shoes and tattered clothes, and his worldly possessions tied in a handkerchief on his back.

In this shabby plight, he presented himself at the telegraph office. He was eyed coldly enough at first, but by and by when tests were given he stood the tests. There was that in the eager eyes and underneath the shabby clothes that could not but make itself felt as a power. He began work. At first, his fellow clerks laughed at him. In time they were won over, and later he stood out as a workman of the first order.

He began to collect about him materials for printing-- machinery without which he never felt quite happy. He did a clever thing one day in the office that brought him to notice. He took a press report at one sitting--a sitting that lasted from 3.30 p.m. till 4.30 a.m.! After that he carefully divided it into paragraphs so that each printer would have exactly three lines to print, and so that a column could be set up in two or three minutes!

It may be that about this time money was rather more plentiful, for Edison began to go to second-hand bookshops and so to gratify his deep-seated thirst for knowledge.

His kindness of heart was well known, and there were many about only too ready to take advantage of it. Some telegraphists roamed the country in time of war--"tramp operators" they were called, who took short engagements and generally ended their time with a "spree." These found out Edison--a man who did not drink himself and a man who might be persuaded to lend them money--and these were his worst enemies.

One day he had bought at an auction fifty volumes of the _North American Review_. Half a dozen men were sponging off him in his rooms when he brought home the books and ranged them unsuspiciously round his walls. Directly he had gone out his guests helped themselves to his purchase, landed them at the nearest pawnbroker's, and drank the money they brought.

But his love for experiments sometimes brought him into scrapes and disaster, as when he moved a bottle of sulphuric acid one day, strictly against rules, and the bottle spilled, the contents eating through the floor to the manager's room below and their eating up _his_ floor and carpet, the unlucky accident bringing Edison his dismissal.

And now, at the age of twenty-one, after many different situations and different experiences, Edison turned his steps to Boston. His openhandedness had left him short of money. As was often the case with him, he was sailing very close to the wind. His dress was poor and shabby, and four days' and nights' traveling had not improved his appearance. When he presented himself at the office where he was to be taken on, the other clerks ridiculed him as "a jay from the woolly west."

They made up their minds to play a practical joke on him. They took the New York telegraph man into their confidence. It was arranged he should send a despatch which Edison was to receive. By this time Edison had so perfected himself in receiving messages that he could write from forty-six to fifty-four words a minute--quicker than any operator in the United States.

Not knowing his man, the sender began slowly--then quickened his pace. So did Edison. Quicker still he worked. Edison was in no way discomfited. Soon the New York man had reached his highest speed, to which Edison responded with ease, cool, collected, and stopping now and then to sharpen a pencil.

He knew by this point that the others were attempting to "get a rise" out of him, but he continued working methodically. He then came to a stop and began to speak softly to the New Yorker.

He said, in his dryly hilarious way, "Say, young guy, change off and send with your other foot."

However, the New Yorker was at his wit's end and had to find someone else to finish. As a result, Edison got his accolades and was afterward highly respected as "the jay from the woolly west."

His position was thereafter in the first row after that. He had now crossed the threshold into manhood and had he realized it, a long, brilliant vision of accomplishment and success stretched before him. Around this time, he experienced a profound, overwhelming conviction regarding his obligations and the chances life presented to him.

I'm going to hustle, Adams, because I have so much to do and because life is so short.

And if we try to look at what he has crowded into a life not long, we must allow he has indeed "hustled" to some purpose. As we briefly glance at the bent of his manhood, his doings fairly dazzle us. He read enormously all sorts of works on telegraphy and electricity, and he produced from his brain that which makes him the greatest inventor of the age. If we tried to enumerate his inventions the names alone would fill pages. We can do little more than naming a few. Among the first of these was how to send four messages at the same time over one telegraph wire.

But even after he had embarked on the glorious sea of discovery, what "ups and downs"--what sea-saws of fortune were in store for him! Hunger at times, torn clothes, and battered shoes. But from depths and half-drowning up again he always came to the surface. He rose grandly, relying on his own indomitable will. About this time good fortune befell him. For inventing some telegraphic appliances he got 50,000 dollars, or rather more than £10,000. He could hardly believe his good luck, and it was with this he immediately rigged up for himself a workshop.

And now he was rapidly rising, and the field before him was gradually opening up wider and wider. He started a laboratory at a place called Newark, and from this time onwards his inventions seemed to flow from his brain in a well-nigh continuous stream.

His workmen were devoted to his service. His genial good-humor and kindliness, the absence of all harshness in his manner, and his love of fun could not but endear him to them. They caught the infection, too, of his earnestness. When he had an idea in his brain he worked at it, as it were, red-hot, almost without rest or cessation, and they were rarely reluctant to help him.

He would lock himself and his crew in a room on the top floor and yell, "Now, you fellas! I've locked the door, and you'll have to stay here until this task is finished."

He may go without eating or sleeping for as much as sixty hours as his brain worked nonstop to complete the task. Then he would unwind and sleep for as many as 36 hours straight.

His fame had since grown immensely. People in Menlo Park, California, where he relocated and which is about 24 miles from New York, began to refer to him as a wizard or a man with magical abilities. They got the impression that he could do anything. Exaggerated rumors about his amazing abilities circulated throughout the nation.

He said, after being surrounded in Newark, "If people track me here, I'll just have to go into the woods."

The brainchild of the inventor produced child after child. As many as forty-five were born at one point in a short period.

There was the Microphone, which is much like the Telephone, except that in the Microphone the sound is magnified. There was the Megaphone, which brings far-away sounds near so that cattle crunching grass six miles off could be heard distinctly at Menlo Park! There was the Kinetoscope we all know, which by swiftly passing pictures--as many as forty-six a second--seems to give us a single person in motion, somewhat on the lines of that toy of our childhood, "The Wheel of Life." And there was the grand king of inventions--the Phonograph--that overtops all the rest.

By this point, we all are aware of it. We have listened to it while holding the tubes to our ears to hear someone speaking far away or the melodies of a song sung by a talented singer.

Edison shipped his first phonogram to England via steamship in 1888. The wax cylinder just needed to be removed, placed in the friend's machine, and set in motion for him to get the sensation that Thomas Edison was in the room conversing with him.

Great men all over the world recorded their astonishment and their praises of the wonderful invention. The Queen sent him a message of congratulation. People flocked to every exhibition to see it--the French ones from countries all over Europe. They saw it and straightway went into raptures. Edison himself, looking into the future, seemed to see volumes it might yet be brought to do. It might be used to write letters merely from dictation. It might be used to make clocks speak--to tell when it was time to come to meals. It might be used for toys. A tiny phonograph might be placed inside a doll, and it would straightway "talk"; or in a toy animal, and it would grunt and growl!

What a strange thing that in this world of passing-away and change we should be able to preserve from destruction such treasures sheltered in a wax cylinder--some great man's words of wisdom, or the silver tones of a sweet musician!

The more Edison's brain accomplished the more did it seem able to do. As a man, he showed himself as untiring as when a boy. He went on discovering. He invented a way of telegraphing from a moving train. He invented an Electric Railroad, that drew delighted thousands at the Chicago Exhibition.

His focus shifted to lighting in 1879, and he focused all of his efforts on developing the incandescent lamp, a type of electric light. He labored nonstop for days at a time. He started on October 16th, but setbacks and accidents appeared to be endangering his idea.

In a fit of ecstasy, he yelled to his partner, "Let us. Let us make a lamp before we sleep, or die trying." It was completed on the morning of the 21st!

The entire globe was astounded. For men everywhere, including miners and divers, it created new opportunities.

On the occasion of its exhibition, people flocked from all parts of the United States. Special trains were run. The same furor over the marvel reigned at the Paris Exposition and every other exhibition. And through it all--fame, popularity enough to turn the head of most mortals--the man remained the same--modest, simple, unpretentious.

From Menlo Park, he went to Orange. His laboratory there was fitted up with everything conceivable that an inventor red-hot and eager might want at a moment's notice. And yet often the workrooms presented the strangest appearance of disorder. Workmen sometimes stretched on benches or floor after a heavy strain, the great master himself thrown down--a stick under his head, a coat wound round it for a pillow, and so snatching a short interval of sleep! He will not be interrupted by visitors. In this great world of his own, he seems at times to live a sort of separate existence.

We are astounded at the incredible accomplishments one man has made in his lifetime and are dazzled and amazed by them. He has not been satisfied with simply taking something, altering it, making it better, and putting it to a new user as persons who are known as inventors have done throughout history. But it appears that he made a direct appeal to the powers of nature to carry out his will. It's almost as if he used the wind, air, sound, and electricity to his advantage.

Rarely does a man spend the rest of his life basking in the glory of a single discovery?
This man is still in his prime, therefore it's impossible to predict what innovations will yet astound us from his mind. We are also unable to comprehend even a small portion of what he has accomplished. He alternates between living in Orange and his house in the north, New Jersey.

As an adult, he exhibits the same friendly sympathy and modesty that as a young man never failed to capture the hearts of his fellow clerks. These things tie his employees to him in loving bonds today. Even though people now celebrate and laud him all over the world, he continues to treat his name and celebrity with the same good-natured indifference that he has displayed throughout. And he still possesses all of the tenacity that helped him as a child gets through long nights of watching television and hard labor. This is a man who, in the words of one source, "has kept the way to the patent office red-hot with his footsteps—this wonder-worker of the modern world."